The Art of War

The Warrior Series: Book One.

The Art of War

Sun Tzu: In Plain English

D.E. Tarver

Writers Club Press
San Jose New York Lincoln Shanghai

The Art of War
Sun Tzu: In Plain English

Writers Club Press
an imprint of iUniverse, Inc.

For information address:
iUniverse, Inc.
5220 S. 16th St., Suite 200
Lincoln, NE 68512
www.iuniverse.com

Any similarities with other translations are strictly coincidental.

ISBN: 0-595-22472-5

Printed in the United States of America

Dedicated to
The United States Marine Corps,
And to the Men and Women who serve God,
Country, and Corps.

"Great leaders aren't great because they fix a lot of problems; they are great because they avoid a lot of problems."

CONTENTS

FOREWORD

Not much is known about the life of Sun Tzu. He may not have lived at all. If he did, it was about 2500 years ago, give or take half a millennium. Some believe he was a general named Sun Wu, maybe so, maybe not. No one can really know at this point, but it doesn't matter. The fact is, the work *The Art of War*, is a masterpiece of strategic literature. The work itself has stood the test of over 2000 years and is still going strong.

Whether he is fact or fiction, his name is synonymous with success. If you want to succeed, you will take the time to learn this material.

PREFACE

Sun Tzu's ideas have been the cornerstone of every great success story since it was written, around 2500 years ago. It should be a central part of your library and way of thinking for business, military, or day-to-day affairs.

This interpretation of *The Art of War* is written in plain English. It does not bog down with flowery, philosophical, or tedious writing. There is no beating around the bush. Strategy is strategy, and the same principles are used whether you are fighting for success or for survival. All organizations, whether predator or prey, function by these same principles no matter their size. I could have added fifty pages of personal dribble or opinion, but I chose to leave the text the way I think it was intended.

This book is laid out like a planning guide and is intended for easy use and implementation.

You are where you are in life because you are shrewd. You are interested in this book because you are aggressive. You want to win, and this book can help you. In any conflict, someone will win and everyone else will lose. There is no "everyone wins" scenario; someone always comes out on top. There is no middle ground. You either do it, or you don't. If you do not understand this you should not be a leader. If you do, this book will show you how to win.

ACKNOWLEDGEMENTS

Special thanks goes to Lisa Anderson, and Shirl Thomas.

Lisa

Thanks for all the hours you spent laboring on this project trying to make me look good.

Shirl

Your hard work and dedication to excellence shines forth in every thing you do.

INTRODUCTION

I have studied Sun Tzu's work most of my life. I have read more translations than I can remember, and almost without exception have found most of them left me wanting something more.

Writers seem to want to sound like an ancient Chinese mystic when they approach a subject like Sun Tzu. When, in reality, what really matters is the lessons themselves. War is the perfect training ground for teaching these lessons because it cuts through so many of our ideas of political correctness and places everything in black and white terms. The old saying, "It doesn't matter if you win or lose, it's how you play the game" goes right out the window when your life is on the line.

So too, in most areas of life, we tend to encumber ourselves with so many rules and ideas of political correctness that we oftentimes lose the whole point of what we'd started out to accomplish. Political correctness and war are not proper bedfellows.

I have taught martial arts, fighting, and self defense most of my life. I can tell you from firsthand experience that, when it's you or him, you'd better make up your mind it's going to be him. Bite, scratch, throw, insult, spit at, punch, kick, or shoot—whatever you have to do to survive, that's what you do. If you don't you die, or worse someone you love dies.

What I most enjoy about Sun Tzu is that *The Art of War* is as much about love, as it is about aggression. The instructions on how to treat your own troops, employees, or family members are laid out in contrast to how you treat your opponent's. You should be filled with love and integrity with one, and completely cunning and manipulative with the other—basic human nature whether we want to admit it or not, and as it should be.

All of nature operates on these same principles, and it is foolish to believe that when push comes to shove we are any different. Watch a pride of lions sneak through the underbrush and surround their prey. They are very cunning. They move into place quietly and take their individual positions without being seen. They then pounce and work as a team, taking down their victims. They mercilessly kill their prey by ripping it apart, and then very gently and lovingly feed their young.

We have to balance out ethics with our nature. Most of us, myself included, don't want to harm anyone. We want everyone to have whatever they want, and for peace and happiness to reign. But the fact remains that we must grow or die.

In writing this book, I wanted to bring the lessons of Sun Tzu out in basic black and white, because that is the way of war. I tried to write in the way Sun Tzu would have if he lived today. I added little conjecture, footnotes, or commentaries about what Sun Tzu really meant. I think the body of work speaks for itself. I didn't so much concern myself with exact word-for-word translation, but tried instead to bring out the whole of his ideas. For example in Book Four, on temperament, the original text reads, "Lifting an autumn hair is no sign of immense strength." In this translation I simply wrote, "To lift a small thing requires no great strength." It contains the same meaning, and the same thought, but it's easier to understand. I did not want to go on and on about what he meant by, "an autumn hair." I only want to know what he meant, and how it applies to me.

I promise you that at no time will I challenge you to snatch the pebble from my hand, nor will I call you grasshopper. I will teach you how to win and how to apply the lessons of Sun Tzu to your life.

The Art of War

D.E. Tarver

www.detarver.com

PLANNING

Conflict is essential to the development of a person, or a people. In its borders are found life and death, success and destruction. You face conflict in everything you do. You must understand it. You must study it thoroughly.

When you have to defend yourself, or before you commit to aggressive action, you must compare yourself to your opponent in five basic ways:

1. Moral Authority
2. Atmosphere
3. Risk
4. Experience
5. Policy

Moral Authority

If you have the moral authority to challenge your opponent and your troops know and believe this, then you will all act and think in the same way. All will work for the common goal. Everyone will be fully engaged and motivated to win. Your troops will believe in you and you can trust them with your life. Heaven will assist you, and nothing can stop you.

If you do not have the moral authority, or if your troops do not believe you do, then you will lose. If you are not absolutely certain of the rightness of your action, or of the faith of your troops, do not engage your opponent or he will destroy you. Wait until you can build a solid image in your community and among your troops. Examine yourself first. Everything begins with you. If you are strong and honest you will have a strong and honest organization. If you are evil and a liar your organization will be filled with evil liars, and you will have to watch your back every second.

Atmosphere

Is the timing right? Is your opponent in a place of weakness—or strength? Are his troops or his subjects disheartened—or joyous? Are they standing in the rain—or in the sunshine? Are the elements working in your favor, or in your opponents? Will you be able to keep your troops supplied with everything they need to win? Can you modify your plan without notice in order to continue??

Think carefully over these things. Once you begin there is no resting. In the end there will be a winner—and a loser. If the timing is right go forth; if it is not, then wait for a more suitable time.

Risk

What are the dangers? Will the path to success be traveled with ease or with difficulty? Will it be open, or narrow and constricted? What is the worst that can happen? What are your chances of survival? What are your chances of death?

Weigh the risks carefully. Are you willing to pay what you could lose in exchange for what you could gain? If not then stop, because you will not be committed to your action and you will lose. It is easy to be committed to an idea. It is hard to stay committed to a process.

Experience

Examine yourself without ego. How much wisdom do you really have? Do your troops see you as wise, credible, benevolent, courageous, and disciplined? Do your troops see you as stern but fair? How do you know? Do you dispense praise and discipline with an even hand to all? Do you delegate authority based on ability—or favoritism? Do you trust those to whom you have delegated to get the job done, or do you constantly look over their shoulders? If they have gained your trust, then trust them. If they have not, then they should not hold a position of authority.

How do your opponent's troops measure him on this same scale? Be absolutely certain of your answer. If you judge wrong here you will be destroyed.

Policy

Examine your troops. Are they divided into proper ranks? Are your leaders strong? Are they respected? How do they measure up to the guidelines for experience? Is each unit properly supplied? Do they have everything they need to get their jobs done? Are you ready and able to keep their needs met? Are you sure of your supply chain? Any weak link could mean defeat. Commit these things to policy, and then follow it evenly and without question. If you are inconsistent with your policy, your troops will lose respect for you and they will not go out of their way for you. You must apply the policy evenly to everyone. If you show even the slightest favoritism in its application you will not be trusted. If someone breaks policy then confront him with the facts. If you do not you will be seen as weak and will lose the respect of your troops.

Every leader should understand these five basic principles. If you know them, and commit them to heart, and act on them in sincerity—then you will win. If you do not, you will be destroyed. You should act from the integrity of your heart. If you are a liar your troops will know, and they will have no respect for you. They will not fight for you and they may even seek your destruction.

In comparing yourself to your opponent, you should examine the following questions very carefully.

1. Who is most in line with Moral Authority? Who is the most popular among their troops and with the people of the land?
2. Which leader has the most experience and talent?
3. Who does the atmosphere and timing favor?
4. Whose policy and discipline are most consistent? Whose troops are most engaged? Whose troops are most discontented?
5. Which organization is stronger in terms of motivation, policy, and esprit de corps? Whose vision and goals are most clear?
6. Whose leaders and troops have the best training?
7. Who is the most evenhanded and consistent with reward, and with punishment? Whose system of reward and punishment is most fairly and clearly understood by its troops?

If you study these basic principles, I can tell you who will win. Do not kid yourself. This is very simple. The leader who commits these things to heart and lives accordingly will conquer. The leader who does not, will be destroyed—or done away with.

Using each element of this strategy you should then take the advantage and start the momentum in your favor. Make each step behind the scenes in order to turn the atmosphere in your direction.

Remember all conflict is based on deception. So when active, you should appear inactive. When planning, you should appear uninterested. When ready for action, you should appear disorganized. Make your opponent think you are where you are not, and never let him know where you are until it is no longer avoidable; then strike with all your force and crush him.

If he has little or no moral authority then plant doubt among his troops and make them think your cause is more righteous. Find where he is least popular and exploit it, and feed the animosity of his detractors. Set one party against another within his camp by finding his weakest leaders and pointing to them as the example of his leadership. Ridicule him and provoke him to anger. Find an area where he has been unfair in discipline or inconsistent in policy and use it to tear down his authority. If he becomes angry, then push him harder. If he grows weary, then give him no rest. Attack when he is least prepared. Appear when he least expects you.

If his army is strong and impenetrable then be prepared for him. Evade him and be very careful. He may be lying in wait to devour you. If you are unsure on any point, then do not attack because you will be destroyed. Focus on your organization. Make sure you are strong on all points. If you are vulnerable when you are attacked you may be destroyed. Regardless of what your opponent says you should always assume that he is planning to attack you. Be prepared at all times. Make sure you are in line with heaven and pray for favor.

If you take all of these things into consideration, then proper planning means you will win, little planning means you will lose, and a failure to plan at all means you will be destroyed.

With these principles we can forecast the outcome of the conflict.

PREPARATIONS

Before you launch your attack you should well consider the overall expense of the campaign. A long operation will be very costly. Make sure you have the money as well as the supplies and the willingness to use them. Give the strike force leaders what they need, but be careful not to give them too much lest they grow overconfident. A person with a full belly moves slowly, but a person who is starving has no strength. Consider every facet of the operation, including the expense of day-to-day operations at home. Make sure you have accounted for every possible scenario and that you have the resources above and beyond normal expenses. Only then should you consider moving forward.

Lay your plans very carefully. Have you done everything behind the scenes that you possibly can? Have you exploited your opponent's weaknesses? Have you set him on edge? The more you tear him down beforehand, the easier the battle will be.

The main objective is a speedy resolution to the engagement. No matter how much planning you have done or how much money you have, a long drawn out conflict will exhaust your organization. Your troops will grow weary and lose their motivation and focus. They will lose their trust in you because it will be evident that you were unprepared. Once your finances run low and your troops are lethargic, your opponent, or some other organization, will move in and exploit your situation and devour you. You will be helpless to defend yourself because you have wasted your money and energy foolishly.

If you cannot see an end to the conflict, then do not attack. You have not worked properly to set the stage for victory.

No one has ever benefited from a drawn out conflict, except the scavengers who feed at the edges. We have all heard examples of armies or people rushing to attack before they were properly prepared. Usually we hear of their defeat. We laugh at them and talk about how foolish they were. But then afterwards, someone else will go out and make almost the exact same mistake. Successful organizations seldom, if ever, engage in long drawn out campaigns. The wisest leaders set the stage for victory and then pounce out of nowhere and consume their prey.

Take as much time as you need behind the scenes. There is no rush when planning. This is the place to be slow and methodical. Do you trust everyone at your planning table? If not, either remove them or control the information they receive. Develop a strong team to keep your strike force supplied with what they need when they need it. There is nothing worse than running out of ammunition in the middle of a firefight.

Once you have launched your attack be very careful not to drain away your substance from your home organization. If you place too heavy a burden on your troops at home they will lose their focus and your organization will suffer. It is wiser to forage off of the opponent. What you have conquered you should consume. Highly reward those who take ground. Make a show of it. Quickly punish those who have hindered the operation. Contrary to popular belief, it is not always better to reward openly and to punish in private. At times a sharp word or a rebuke out in the open will do more good than a reward, but only the best leaders have the instinct for this. The reward must be appropriate for the accomplishment. Too much reward will make it appear too easy; too little will make it seem not worth the effort. Discipline as well must be appropriate and justified. Too harsh a punishment will make others afraid to take chances—too easy and they will be undisciplined.

Replace the opponent's emblems with your emblems. Treat their troops well. Reward them, pay them and promise them security. They will fight hard to earn your trust and some of them may prove to be more valuable than your own troops. They will speak well of you to your opponent's troops and cause discord in his ranks. After your victory you should absorb everyone you can, and give them security and benefit and they will become valuable assets.

Remember, once you attack, your objective is victory, not a long fight.

Be wise. You are the leader. The fate of your army and of your troops rests squarely on your shoulders. Whether you conquer, or survive, or are disseminated depends on you and your understanding of this strategy.

OFFENCE

Protect your own organization first. Be certain you are strong in every aspect. This is of supreme importance.

To destroy your enemy in head-to-head battle is not the best way to win. It is much better to break his spirit and crush his will to fight, and to take your opponents troops without harming them or causing harm to yourself. This should be achievable if you have prepared properly. Once your opponent feels at ease, bring him into your plan and use what you can accordingly.

Practically speaking, it is always best to conquer your opponent without violence, by cutting off his strategy. The next best strategy is to destroy your opponent's ability to fight. Third best is to fight him head on. The worst plan of all is to attack his strongholds and fortifications.

As a rule, never attack a stronghold if you can possibly avoid it. It will take entirely too much time and could stretch your resources out too thinly. An impatient leader will send his troops and resources streaming toward a fortification, which will result in his losing a third of his men and a third of his recourses for nothing. The stronghold will remain. Such are the risks of a siege.

Attack the weak areas. Wear down his resolve. When he is weak or distracted, start picking apart the stronger areas. The skillful leader seduces the opponent's troops without a fight. He takes control of the opponent's strongholds without a frontal assault, and he replaces the leadership of the entire organization without wasting his own resources. His goal is to assimilate the whole organization by means of offensive strategic planning and without the use of his own troops or resources. This is the art of offense.

When forced to use your own resources, this is the general guideline:

> If you have ten times the strength of your opponent then surround him, and leave no escape and, strangle him.

> If you are five times his strength, then attack him.

> If you are double his strength, then divide his resources and attack each part separately with your full force.

> If you are equally matched, then you may advance only after you have completely planned out your strategy.

> If you are weaker, you must be faster and capable of outmaneuvering him.

> If in all areas you are completely overpowered, then be elusive, defensive, and ready to snap at him. Then run away.

In general, a small force is but a trophy for a larger one, so you must be prepared to fiercely defend against his inquires.

Now there are three ways in which an organization can bring calamity to its own attack force.

1. If a command is issued out of ignorance, such as ordering an advance or a retreat out of time without knowing the attack force's complete situation. If you do this you will cut their feet out from under them.

2. If ignorant of even the smallest part of their own strategy, interfering with their administration, or attempting to apply the same logic to the strike force that is applied to the home organization. To do so would confuse the strike force leaders and cause them to doubt your ability and your wisdom.

3. By placing an incompetent person, or even a person of slightly lesser ability, in charge of a strike force. This appointment should be made strictly on the basis of ability, and nothing personal should enter into this decision. Use your intuition. Appoint the strongest leader, not the strongest workhorse. A wrong decision can destroy the confidence of your troops and can cause your defeat before you even start.

If you have not strictly followed these principles, then your army will become restless and distrustful. A shrewd predator will see this and attack you. This will bring chaos to your strike force and to your organization and will cast victory far away from you. Any betrayal, on any level of your organization, is completely unacceptable and must be dealt with swiftly and sternly. Make an example of the traitor, and closely examine those close to him.

Be cunning. Be wise. Develop your intuition and understand the following.

1. Whichever side knows when to fight and when not to fight, will win.

2. Whichever side knows how to best manage their resources, will win.

3. Whichever side has fully engaged their troops and developed the strongest sense of esprit de corps and common purpose, will win.

4. Whichever side is the most patient when preparing and the quickest to seize upon their opponent's mistakes or misfortunes, will win.

5. Whichever strike force has the freedom and resources to conduct the attack without constant interference by the organization, will win.

Remember, know the opponent and know yourself and you will not see defeat even in a hundred conflicts. If you know yourself, but not your opponent, then your chances of winning or losing are uncertain. But even your victories will be very costly. If you do not know yourself or your opponent then you will be in mortal danger every step you take.

TEMPERAMENT

Throughout all of history great leaders secured their home front first. They made their defenses sharp and their organizations strong in everyway. They made themselves impenetrable, and only then did they look outward.

The strength of your army is entirely up to you. Only you can ensure that your troops are fully engaged and that you are united toward a single purpose with the utmost integrity. Are your troops ready to fight to the bitter end if necessary to defend the organization?

Do not concern yourself with the opponent at this stage. Your opponent will consistently offer you many opportunities to destroy him. But do not underestimate him. Great leaders focus on keeping their own army safe first, because no one can guarantee your opponent's defeat.

Remember, just because you know how to win does not necessarily mean you will be able to do so.

Defensive security comes only with strict adherence to strong policy. Defend yourself against a superior opponent; attack a weaker or disorganized opponent. Lead for the good of your troops, not to boost your own ego. Align yourself with heaven, but do not expect heaven to bend to your will, regardless of your passion.

Those skilled in defense can hide in plain sight. They can vanish into the recesses of the earth and remain motionless and undetectable. Those skilled in offence can flash forth out of nowhere, and by the time you see them you are dead. Be a shrewd leader skilled in both defense and offence, and then you will have security as well as proper victory.

Be a leader with vision. To see an opportunity only when it is apparent to everyone is not very impressive, nor is being complimented by everyone with your successes. To lift a small thing requires no great strength, to see only what is right before your face requires no great vision, and to hear the booming roar of thunder requires no great hearing.

The greatest leaders not only win, but win with excellence and with ease. They do not fight to build a reputation, but to win. They are meticulous in their planning and they make no mistakes. Opponents are defeated before they even know they have been attacked. A great leader establishes a position that makes him invincible and never misses the proper time to strike the opponent down.

The greatest strategist seeks battle only after he has already won the conflict. He has done all the work necessary behind the scenes. He has set the trap, and by the time he appears his opponent has already been destroyed. Others, who are destined for destruction, rush into battle relying on their sheer force of will. They have no plan, no strategy, and they spend their time fighting to survive with any notion of victory a distant afterthought.

Those skilled in conflict or warfare have the highest integrity in their hearts. They tell no lies. They spread no rumors. They treat everyone fairly, regardless of personal consequences. They are compassionate, but unyielding. Thus everyone in their army, even those who may disagree with them, trusts them and it is this very trust that gives them the power to control success in all that they do.

The elements of the art of war are these:

You must first understand where you are and where you need to go.

You should know the space between the two points and correctly estimate the quantity of supplies you will need.

You should carefully calculate your plans to make sure you can have everything where you need it when you need it.

Take another look at your opponent and make sure you have not underestimated him.

Compare your army with that of your opponent's all the way down the line, placing everything on the balance scales. If everything is right for the attack, it should be the same as weighing a ton against an ounce.

Motivate your troops and attack with the force of a bursting dam.

FORCE

Generally speaking, controlling many is the same as controlling a few. It is simply a matter of organization. The same strategy is used in motivating a large army as in engaging a small army; it is a matter of proper communication.

To ensure that your army will stand in the day of battle it is important to use both frontal assaults and covert operations. Be certain to have a strong plan and good intelligence. Make sure you have completed all of your work behind the scenes prior to the day of conflict. If you have done everything well and you know your opponent's strong points as well as his weak points, then fighting against his army will be like dropping a ten pound rock on an egg.

During the conflict use the frontal assault to engage the opponent. This is what he expects and he will settle in for battle. Keep him distracted with this while you destroy him with your covert operations. Be clever, because methods of covert operations are as inexhaustible as the stars of heaven or as the sands of the sea. They are never-ending like the flowing of a river or the passage of day into night and into day again.

Do not limit yourself. Use your imagination. There are only a few musical notes, yet more melodies can be created than can ever be heard. There are only a few basic primary colors, yet artists can blend them to create more colors than can ever be seen. There are only a few basic flavors, but a chef can use them the create more flavors than can ever be tasted.

In competition there are only two methods of attack: direct assault and covert operations. The wise leader can combine these two methods to create endless possibilities and strategies. Direct action and covert operations depend on each other like two halves of a circle, and there is no an end to their possibilities.

The force of a torrent can toss boulders, because of its momentum. A hawk can break the back of its prey when it strikes, because of its timing. In war, you should use your covert operations to build momentum for your frontal assault. Let the energy build to the breaking point like a tightly pulled crossbow. Let your timing be like pulling the trigger, and your momentum like the flight of the arrow—straight to the heart and swift and terrible.

The warrior should be shocking in his onset and perfect in his timing. In the midst of the conflict there may seem to be chaos, but he is in complete control. His highly trained and disciplined strike force moves in for the kill while the opponent is running around in circles.

Train your army in simulated chaos, and their discipline will be perfect in battle. Train them in simulated fear, and their courage will not fail. Train them in simulated weakness, and they will become strong. Train them properly, and they will never be taken by surprise. They can appear chaotic yet remain sharp and ordered underneath. They can appear fearful and timid yet contain the courage and energy of a lion. Hiding strength with apparent weakness is covert.

So a skillful leader keeps the opponent on the move by maintaining deceitful appearances. By feigning weakness or disorder he deceives the opponent into attacking or flanking, all the while laying a death trap for him. He offers his opponent bribes or promises to keep him off balance as he prepares his strike force from behind the scenes. He is clever and combines all of his energy into one massive final strike and he does not rely too much on any single element. The force of his final strike is like massive boulders rolling down a steep hill crushing everything in their path.

STRENGTH AND WEAKNESS

Generally speaking, the one who is first to the field of battle has time to rest, while his opponent rushes into the conflict weary and confused. The first will be fresh and alert. The second will waste most of his energy trying to catch up. You should therefore lead your opponent into the conflict and make sure he never leads you. Lead him by making it appear to his advantage to advance. Push him back by inflicting pain. If you control the movement of your opponent you can control his downfall.

If he is trying to rest, bring him to exhaustion. If he is well supplied, cut him off and starve him. If he is trying to lay low until everything blows over, pick at him until he runs. Strike at places that he must swiftly defend. Appear suddenly in places where he is not expecting you. You can move freely about, if you move behind the scenes.

Insure your victory by striking at places where the opponent has not or cannot build defenses. Find his weak areas and apply your strength. Ensure the safety of your organization by checking and rechecking every point until you are certain of your strength. If you have a weakness he will find it, so have no weaknesses.

You will be successful in aggression if your opponent never knows when or where to expect your attack. You will be successful in defense if your opponent never knows when or where to attack.

Master the subtle art of secrecy. It is in the details where you vanish. Become soundless, motionless, and invisible. Be everywhere, but appear nowhere. In this way you will hold your opponent's life in the palm of your hand. From here you can attack at will and overpower your opponent, or you can vanish without worry of pursuit if you are more clever and speedy than he.

When you are ready to strike, remain invisible and draw the opponent out even if he is highly fortified. Start fires and cause emergencies that he must rush to aid, then strike while he is occupied. Break his organization into fractions and devour it one piece at a time. This way you will be able to strike with all of your might against his weakest places, and his life will be worthless.

If you are not ready to fight, you can prevent the opponent from striking at you even though you may be standing clearly in the open. Toss something unexpected into the equation. Even if it is off the wall and makes no sense it will cause him to wonder, to feel nervous and fearful.

Never let your opponent know where or when you intend to attack. Let him worry constantly and make him strengthen all areas at all times. This way he will spread his resources thin, he will be weak in all areas, and you can attack anywhere you choose.

Remember, if you appear to attack the front, he will rush resources from the rear and become much weaker there. If you appear to attack the right, then his left will be weakened. You would do well to keep this in mind as you plan. Gather all of your strength, create a weak spot, and strike with all of your might.

Be very careful that you are not stretched too thinly. If a larger force is planning to attack you, but you do not know where or when the strike is coming, you must be very cunning and find out his plan. Use any means necessary. Make him angry; force him to reveal his true intentions. Search diligently for any weaknesses to exploit. Meticulously compare your army to your opponents, and be as certain as you can that you are using your strength where it will do the most good.

While planning, be absolutely secret. Remember that he is watching you. Conceal yourself and hide any emotion or fear. Appear strong even if you are terrified and he will not be able to read you or figure you out. He will be able only to look to your past to see how you handled similar situations, so make sure you are not following the same old strategy, or he will have you pegged.

Follow the example of water. Water forms to fit whatever container it is in. If it is poured out it forms to the ground and rushes to the lowest or weakest points of that particular terrain, then moves as a single body. It erodes the weak to bring down the strong. In this way water can wash away a mountain.

Avoid your opponent's strength and strike his weakness. Shape your strategy to his nature. Be flexible and moving. Stay in no constant shape. Move as your opponent moves, avoid his strikes, and conform to his strategy. If you can mold yourself to your opponent and outmaneuver him and outthink him and win even though he is stronger, then you will be celebrated as a gift from God.

MANEUVERING

Generally speaking, the principles of conflict management are as follows: The strike force leaders receive their orders from the organization, they assemble their resources, train their troops, set up operations, and jockey for position. Of these, gaining the position of advantage can be, by far, the most difficult.

Maneuvering is made difficult, because you must appear aimless, even though you are moving directly into position. You must bait your opponents to divert their attention while you work feverishly to establish a stronghold. It is even possible to get a late start, to bait your opponent, to create difficulties for him, and to then steal the position of advantage away from him. Anyone who can do this is a master of maneuvering.

Remember that both rewards and risks are intrinsic in maneuvering for position. You should never risk your entire army while maneuvering. Send the strike force forward, keep them well supplied, and give them the proper amount of time to reach their objective. Never rush them, or they will make mistakes and bring disaster down on you. If you push them too hard you will lose your leaders to your opponent. If you act too hastily you will rush forward with your strengths, leaving your weaknesses exposed and vulnerable, then one tenth of what you wanted will cost you ten times what you had planned.

Be very careful about entering into agreements with unknown organizations. If you do not know them, you cannot trust their intentions. If they are weak, you will become weak. If they are strong, they may be planning on devouring you.

It is difficult to advance in an area you know little about. Use advisors who are familiar with these areas. Keep them in your sight, and far from your plans.

Remember, war is based on communication and deception. In your organization and strike force make sure your lines of communication are clear, safe, and understood by those they are intended for. Leak your communications to deceive your opponent. Set the stage carefully. Watch. Listen. Timing is everything. One wrong move can destroy the spirit of your entire army and confuse your strike force leaders, causing them to doubt you. Watch the opponent. When are they strong? When are they weak or distracted?

When are they on guard, and when are they relaxed? Never attack when their spirit is up. Wait until they are not paying attention, then strike as fast as the wind, marching forward as a mighty forest. Invade their camp like wildfire consuming everything you can and then, stand your ground like a mountain. Plunder the spoil to replenish your supplies and reward your troops lavishly. Promote your leaders to govern the new territories. Fortify the positions of advantage, then stop and rework your strategy before you move on. Make sure you have learned everything you can from what you have just been though. Those who learn well from their experiences will continue to be victorious.

Remember these things:

1. Never attack an organization that has better communication or is more motivated than your own.
2. Never attack an organization that holds higher ground. Take the higher ground first, and then attack.
3. Never move forward as the opponent recoils. This could be a trap.

4. Never attack an organization that is more committed to the outcome than you are.

5. Never take the enemies bait.

6. Never continue to attack an opponent who has given up.

It is wise to leave an avenue of retreat to an opponent you have surrounded. Give him the opportunity to quit. Once you have him trapped, be careful not to press him too hard, or he will have no choice but to fight. Desperate opponents fight fiercely. If you press too hard and he beats you, you will have thrown the victory from your own hands and, even if you win, your victory will be extremely costly.

VARIATIONS

Now, we know the military gives the strike force leaders the permission and resources to form a plan, and the strike force consolidates resources and manpower to lead the attack.

While engaged, it is important for the strike force leaders to remember:

1. Do not seek rest in hostile territory.
2. Build solid relations with trusted allies.
3. Never relax when you are isolated.
4. If you are cut off, use your strategy.
5. If you are cornered, fight.

Be careful when planning. Some plans lead to victory, some to destruction. Some paths are easy and some are difficult. There are paths that should be avoided altogether; there are strongholds you should not approach; there are positions of advantage you should leave alone; and there are some rules that you should not heed.

Variations of strategy are endless, but the leaders who have the best understanding overall will have an easier time handling resources and manpower. The leader who does not have a good understanding, even if he is extremely knowledgeable in all other areas, will not likely be able to turn his knowledge into results.

A leader who does not have a good understanding of adaptability or does not know how to make variations in his strategy, even though he understands what is at stake and the advantages, will not be able to unite his troops in times of need.

Therefore, when planning, you should thoroughly consider all advantages and disadvantages in every point of your plan. By concentrating on the advantages you can be aggressive with your strategy. By concentrating on the disadvantages you can alleviate your fears and many of the dangers.

Consider these things:

1. How will you subjugate your opponents?
2. How will you aggravate them?
3. How will you keep them occupied?
4. How will you bait them?
5. How will you maneuver them about?

Remember, never count on the weakness of the opponent, but always on your own strength. Do not place your trust in the opponent's lack of aggression, for he will attack, and if he doesn't, then another will. Believe instead, in your own prowess. Concentrate more on your own fortifications than on your opponent's strengths. After all, you never know if he's bluffing.

There are several faults that can turn an otherwise perfect plan into disaster. These faults are in the leader and are usually barely discernible until they surface. When you assume command, examine yourself and your leaders thoroughly and keep these five things close to your heart:

1. If you are ready to stand your ground to the death you can easily be killed.
2. If you are afraid to fight you can easily be captured.
3. If you cannot control your emotions you can easily be provoked.
4. If you are overly sensitive you can easily be shamed.

5. If you baby your troops you can easily be distressed.

These five areas in leaders are easily manipulated and can ruin an entire campaign. If the strike force fails because of its leadership, the fault will most likely lay in one of these areas.

Keep them always in the forefront of your thoughts, and evaluate your decisions accordingly.

MOBILITY

Once you have gained your position, you must consider properly setting up your organization, as well as the advantage of an overall view. You should quickly pass places where you are highly visible, and seek to set up a base of operations in a place where you can be secret and hide.

Make sure your base is at the highest point, and you will ensure that you never have to climb a mountain in order to fight. Leave that burden to your opponent.

Never set up camp with your back to a river. And, if you must cross a body of water, move far away from it before setting up. Then your opponent will have to cross the water to attack. When they do, attack only after their forces are cut in half by the body of water.

Never set up camp on soft ground. And, if you must pass over soft or shaky ground, do so quickly and do not delay. If you are attacked while on soft ground, stand where the ground is surest and cling to that which you know best. That's about the best you can do under the circumstances.

If you are attacked on a plateau, try to position yourself in a place of easy maneuverability—with a mountain to your right and to your rear. This way, you will not have to worry as much about your rear, because the opponent will come from the front.

By using these kinds of advantages many great leaders have defeated their opponents.

Armies are usually safer in places with a better view of the surrounding territory than in place with less visibility. It is better to have light on a subject than to remain in darkness.

Remain on solid ground. Do not get bogged down in the mud where there is uncertainty and danger. Keep your organization strong and healthy. This will help you gain many victories.

Where there are hills and embankments, strive to remain on the enlightened side with uncertainty behind you. This will be advantageous to you because it is always better to know the lay of the land and to use the natural terrain to your advantage.

If there has been a deluge of activity nearby it will most likely affect the conditions of your strategy. Watch and be absolutely certain before you proceed. It may be necessary to let things die down a bit before you continue. You may need to modify your plan in accordance with what is happening elsewhere.

Should you come across pitfalls—such as rocky or difficult ground, or quicksand—move away from them as fast as you can, and remember where they are. It would be advantageous to trap your enemy in them or use them to keep him off balance while you attack.

Pay close attention to your surroundings. Are there areas that cause you doubt? If so, you must take the initiative to search them diligently. Spies or bushwhackers can hide in ways that are tedious to search. In fact, they use these areas to position themselves for attack.

Watch your surroundings. Pay attention to the activities of your opponent.

If he is close by but remains calm, he is sure of his strength.

If he is farther away and is trying to provoke you, he wants you to advance to a place that is advantageous to him. He is trying to bait you.

If the trees move, he is coming; but if the birds remain still in the undergrowth, he is trying to misdirect you.

If the birds suddenly take flight, he is waiting in ambush. When the small animals are frightened, predators are near.

If the activity in his camp is fast and direct, he is setting up a strike force.

If the activity in his camp is slow and methodical, he is pulling together his resources.

If his words are humble but he continues preparations, he is going to attack.

If his words are strong and he rushes towards you but does not attack, he is feeling you out.

If he moves heavy resources close to his side, he is preparing for battle.

If he seeks an alignment but offers no contract, he is plotting.

If he has a sudden buildup and formations in his camp, he is preparing the way for the strike force.

If he strikes with only half of his force, while the other half moves to the rear, he is trying to lure you into a trap.

If he sees an advantage, but does not take it, he is exhausted.

If he is irritable, he is under stress.

If he consumes his own resources, he is broke.

If his troops gather in small groups and whisper, they have lost their respect and loyalty.

If he is trying to lead by excessive rewards, he is trying to bribe his troops because they have lost their confidence.

If he is driving them through punishments, his troops are at the breaking point, and can be easily turned.

If his messengers come with great swelling compliments, he is preparing to seek a truce.

Now, concerning your own forces, keep this in mind. It is not necessary to always outnumber your opponent, as long as you don't assume an aggressive posture. It is enough to gather your resources, keep your eye on your opponents, and grow. If you have no strategy, and you fail to take threats seriously, you will eventually be devoured.

As you grow, remember: If you punish your people before they are loyal to you, they will rebel. If they rebel, they are useless. So, as you gather people, treat them kindly, teach them your policies and be certain they understand. Then you may control them by strict adherence to the policy, and unify them with activities. When your policy is enforced evenly, everyone will accept it. If it is carried out sporadically or with favoritism, no one will accept it. You should show great confidence in your people, but always insist on your orders being followed. Tell them what you want and let them figure out how to do it. You will be amazed with their plans, and everyone will benefit.

TERRAIN

Terrain is a very important part of any conflict, and to win a battle you must understand your terrain. Generally speaking, there are six different types of terrain you must be familiar with. They are:

1. Accessible
2. Entrapping
3. Stalemated
4. Narrow
5. Steep
6. Distant

Accessible Areas

Accessible ground has plenty of room and is easily reached by either side. It is important to be there first and occupy the choice areas. Claim the higher, sunny ground from where you can see your opponent approach. When it is wide open, however, it will be hard to defend and will cost you a great sum if attacked, but you will have the advantage. Remember that you are in an open area and should protect your supply lines at all cost.

If you don't take the higher ground you may be surrounded and cut off.

Entrapping Areas

Entrapping ground gives you easy access for advancement, but makes it nearly impossible to return. It is similar to running down a mountain to fight, and then having to run back up it to retreat. Make certain your opponent is not ready for battle before you strike, and you will win. If he is prepared however, and you fail to destroy him, you will have no retreat and you may be destroyed.

Stalemated Areas

Stalemated grounds are where either side will pay heavily for the first move. If you are in this situation your opponent will try to bait you, and you should ignore him. Better yet, pull back and see if he will advance. If he advances, strike when his troops are strung out half the distance, thus giving you the advantage.

Narrow Areas

Narrow ground is dangerous; you must get there first to set up traps and ambushes, and then wait patiently for the opponent to walk into them. If your opponent is there first, do not advance. You must entice him out and kill him. If you arrive at the same time with roughly equal forces, attack him.

Steep Areas

Steep ground can cause heavy loses. Make sure you are there first and take the higher ground. Then your opponent must struggle uphill to reach you, and you will have a great advantage. If your opponent is there first, do not attack, because you will face severe loses. You must entice him out to fight him, or leave him alone.

Distant Areas

Distant ground is where the enemy is far away. If your opponent is a great distance from you and has roughly the same resources, it is not advisable to attack. The cost associated with conducting a battle at a great distance is exorbitant and, even if you are victorious, you will profit little.

In addition to the six terrains, there are also six common faults among leaders that can cause you defeat. You should examine yourself carefully as you study each one.

1. Flight
2. Defiance
3. Decline
4. Collapse
5. Chaos
6. Defeat

Flight

Flight is when a leader miscalculates his odds because he is rushed, and sends his troops in to attack a force even up to ten times his size. The result will be the retreat of your forces and you will lose the confidence of your troops.

Defiance

Defiance happens when the leaders are too weak to control the troops. The troops will not take them seriously and will not obey orders.

Decline

Decline happens when the leaders are too harsh and the troops are not well cared for. The organization will decline because your troops will have no spirit and will put forth no initiative.

Collapse

Collapse happens when your strike force leaders are overly confident, angry, or proud and tip their hand or charge into battle before the organization has determined if the timing is right.

Chaos

Chaos occurs when your strike force leaders are weak and have no authority. They fail to delegate properly and do not hold their leaders accountable for their responsibilities. The troops have no clear chain of command and do not fully understand their jobs.

Defeat

Defeat occurs when your leaders are unaware of their opponent's size or power, yet launch ahead with a strike against a vastly superior force.

It is the responsibility of the leaders to take the time to work up a great strategy. You should give your troops an honest and solid plan. Let them know of the dangers and difficulties up front. Tell them as much as you can about their opponent and what they are about to face. Then, even if they are cut off from the organization, they may still be able to bring about a victory.

Be a leader who does not seek fame. Know when to retreat without concern of losing face. Keep only the good of the organization in your heart and you will be more valuable to the organization than a priceless jewel. Love your troops like children and they will follow you through hell. Love them like your own children and they will die for you. Be careful not to indulge them and always be strict and evenhanded with discipline, or they will become like spoiled children and will be useless.

If you know that you are ready to attack, but do not know the condition of your opponent, then you are only half done with your planning.

If you know the condition of your opponent, but do not fully know the condition of your own troops, then you are only half done with your planning.

If you know the condition of your opponent, and know that you are ready, but have not studied the terrain, then you are only half done with your planning.

Keep these things close to your heart and, once you charge, you will never be turned back.

If you know your opponent and you know yourself, victory will always be close at hand.

SITUATIONS

As in all things on earth, there are various basic situations in which you may find yourself. While the scenarios are endless, you should carefully study the following nine. They are:

1. Dispersed—when organizations war within their own territory
2. Borderline—when you penetrate your opponent's territory, but stick close to the borders
3. Contentious—territory that is highly prized by either two or more opponents
4. Exposed—territory where more than one organization has free reign
5. Intersection—territory used as a gateway to reach the masses
6. Critical—territory you have entered deeply enough that there is danger of you being trapped
7. Difficult—territory where penetration is very costly or risky
8. Pressed—territory where you have had difficulty penetrating, but where your opponent can attack at leisure and without great expense
9. Deadly—when you are in positions where you must fight with all you have or die

When in any of these situations, the instructions are simple. Never fight on dispersed territory; never stay long in borderline territory; never openly attack in contentious territory; never stand alone in exposed territory; form strong allies in intersecting territory; gather and reserve resources in critical territory and, when pressed, stay on the move; in deadly territory fight with all of your heart and resources.

A skillful strike force leader knows to divide his opponent's forces for easier attack. He knows to disrupt the opponent's communications and supplies. He separates the opponent's strengths and weaknesses and penetrates the weak areas before the opponent can rescue them. He tears down the motivation of his opponent's forces and makes his leaders look foolish. He finds a way to disrupt even the strongest of his opponent's alliances. He looks for ways to destroy his opponent's morale. He knows when to take the advantage and the advance, and he knows when to stop, when to shut up, and when to listen.

When threatened with imminent attack, seize something that is of value to the opponent, and he will stop and negotiate with you. If you take advantage of your opponent's mistakes, then you must advance with speed and come from nowhere to exploit his weaknesses.

When attacking, it is vitally important for your leaders and troops to function at their absolute best. Remember:

1. When you are in danger, your troops will unite and work diligently.
2. Your troops must trust that their needs will continuously be met.
3. Do not cause undue stress among your troops. Conserve your strength.
4. Move undetected and plan secretly.

Let your troops know when the situation is desperate, and they will fight to the death with you. At first, fear may cease them, and they may weep, but when the day of reckoning comes, they will stand tall and fight with all they have. They will show strength, unity, and determination to your opponent, they will remain vigilant beyond their discipline; they will remain devoted beyond what you ask; they will remain faithful beyond your promises of reward; and they will remain trustworthy beyond your supervision.

Do away with all rumors immediately and clear up any misconceptions, so they will focus entirely on the task at hand. You will be like a snake with fangs at each end. If attacked at either end, the other end will strike. If attacked in the middle, both ends will attack at the same time. All the parts of your organization will function as one; even mortal enemies who find themselves on the sea in a storm will work together for mutual advantage.

The very reason leaders exist is to assemble men and resources and lead them through difficult situations. Adapting to changing situations and understanding the human psyche is your nature and mission in life. Set the example for courage and all will strive to reach that standard.

As the leader, you should lead your organization as though leading one person by the hand. Remain quiet to maintain secrecy. Act with integrity and fairness to maintain discipline. Even your most trusted troops should know only part of your plan. Remain aloof and mysterious in your strategy. Be ready to change directions at any moment. Embrace the new, change the old, and never remain stagnant.

Sometimes, at a critical moment, when your strategy is solid and your goals are clear it may be necessary to go for broke. If this is the case, you should act like a man who has climbed a mountain and cut his rope. Drive your army headlong toward the goal—burn your bridges, commit your resources, and only then tip your hand. Put yourself in a situation where your troops believe they must reach the goal to survive. This is the work of a master leader.

Now as you invade new territory, you will find all nine situations. When you find yourself on:

1. Dispersed ground, unify your troops;
2. Borderline ground, insure communications;

3. Contentious ground, keep your lines tight;

4. Exposed ground, guard for defense;

5. Intersecting ground, strengthen alliances;

6. Critical ground, insure supply lines;

7. Difficult ground, press onward quickly;

8. Pressed ground, cut off retreat;

9. Deadly ground, explain the situation to your troops and fight with all your heart and soul.

It is human nature to fight when pressed, to fight desperately when surrounded, and to sharpen vigilance when in danger.

Before you consider leading an attack, make sure you know the territory well. Prevent or disrupt your opponent's alliances to keep them from standing against you in force.

Reward your troops when they are not expecting it. Do this with craft and you can lead ten thousand troops as easily as a single man. Keep them aware of dangers and they will stay sharp. To kill an enemy, you must be close, and in being close you face the most danger. Be strict with your disciplines and follow your plans, and you will destroy the opponent in the long run.

When you launch an attack, be sure to seal your borders, destroy all passes, and cut off access to your headquarters where you deal with secret matters. In meetings, be stern and straightforward with what you expect.

Be helpful and polite to your opponent. Smile and giggle like a shy young virgin until he lets down his guard; then rush forward and take his life.

FIRE

When in battle, you must engage the opponent with all fierceness and malice. Although you should have mercy on his troops, you should have no concern for the organization itself. Fire can be an awesome weapon, or an excellent diversion.

There are five basic uses for fire when attacking: burning troops, burning supplies, burning tools, burning warehouses, and burning weapons. In these uses, fire is a powerful weapon, but the time and conditions must be right for its use, and you must have the proper tools and training to use it.

Watch the seasons. The best conditions are when the weather is dry and a light wind is blowing.

Generally speaking, fire is used to stir up the opponent's troops. If fire is set within the opponent's camp, rush in from the outside and attack. If, however, the opponent's troops are not shaken, then do not attack. Instead set back and bide your time. If the timing is right when the fire hits its peek, attack if it is safe to do so, but if not, stay put. Your attack should be so fierce that it crushes the opponent's fighting spirit; but be very careful and remember that you are attacking a cornered prey.

If it is possible to start a fire yourself, then wait for the best time and attack. Gather all of your resources and manpower. Set the stage carefully. It may be wise to cause another diversion to distract your opponent, then set the fire to cause him much distress, and then attack with all ferocity and speed. Make sure you never attack from the same direction the fire is going, attack where the fire has already been.

The exact time for using fire must be well planned. Once planned, carefully watch the seasons and the conditions to be sure the atmosphere remains favorable.

If you use fire to set the stage for an attack, you must be wise and cautious. If you use water to aid your attack it must be powerful, and remember that water is used only to cut off troops and resources, and never for plunder.

It would be very foolish of you to employ your troops to fight and finally win the conflict, and then horde the rewards. You should lavishly reward merit; make a show of it, and your future will be bright.

Never attack if there is no gain. Never let your anger provoke you to useless conflict. Fight only for justice, gain, or defense. Never engage your strike force simply to puff up your ego. If it is to your advantage to move forward, then do so. If it is not, remain where you are.

Always remember, regardless of your current emotions, anger will give way to joy, and stress will give way to peace. But if you launch forth foolishly and destroy your own army it will never return, nor can the dead ever be brought back to life.

SPIES

Strike force operations are always very expensive to an organization. It may take years of planning and millions of dollars and countless hours of preparations for a battle that will last for only a single day. With this in mind, it is stupid to refuse to pay for information that may save you time and energy—as well as the lives of your men. Remember, your troops have families and children and lives outside of your organization. It is inhumane for you to force them to labor needlessly, and it is much more expensive. One who would do such a thing is not a good leader, nor is he wise in the handling of resources.

Great leaders achieve goals that are beyond the dreams of everyday men because they understand how to bend people's wills and gain insight into an opponent's secrets. This insight can never be gained by the use of mediums or spirits. No amount of experience or deductive reasoning will ever tell you what your opponent is planning. The only way to gain this type of insight is from other people who have firsthand knowledge of the facts.

This is where spies come in. Basically, there are five types of spies with which you must be familiar.

1. Indigenous spies
2. Inside spies
3. Converted spies
4. Counter spies
5. Tactical spies

Indigenous Spies

Indigenous spies are ordinary people who live in and around the opponent's center of influence. Indigenous spies may not know what your opponent is planning, but they can see what he is doing, and they can give you a feel for the kind of support your opponent is getting from the general public.

Inside Spies

Inside spies are people placed in or around leadership positions of the opponent's organization. They are usually discontented with their positions and seeking fortune. Approach them privately and bribe them. When you are absolutely sure you are done with them, do away with them. They cannot be trusted.

Converted Spies

Converted spies are spies the opponent has sent to spy on you, and having been compromised, you send them back as a double agent. Use them for whatever you need, but never trust them.

Counter Spies

Counter spies are people expert in counter intelligence. They get misinformation into the hands of the opponent. Give them time to plan, and the tools they need. Deception is sometimes more valuable than information.

Tactical Spies

Tactical spies are those who gather information on the ground and report back to you with it. They penetrate the opponent's sphere of influence and gather information by being crafty. They are very loyal by nature. Treat them well.

Some of the most important people in your organization's strategy are spies. A good spy can save you countless hours and untold fortunes; therefore they should be rewarded most lavishly. Of all of your strategy and planning, no secret is as vital as espionage.

In dealing with spies you must know how to read people to be sure of their loyalty. You should treat good spies with much kindness, but you should always be straightforward with them. This is a delicate matter.

If one of your spies leaks delicate information, it is imperative that both the spy and the people he told be killed.

Regardless of the plan of attack it is always necessary to know as much as you can about the leaders of the opponent's organization.

You must be relentless at finding enemy spies in your own organization. Once you find them: pay them, bribe them, give them expensive gifts, threaten them—do whatever is necessary to turn them into converted spies so that you can use them. These converted spies can, in turn, bring you inside spies and can also be used to carry misinformation back to the opponent. The purpose of all espionage is to acquire knowledge, and the inside spy is the source of the best knowledge, so treat them very well.

Spies are the cornerstones of any successful victory. It is with their information that you move, act and plan.

The Art of Warfare
Sun Pin: In Plain English

D.E. Tarver
www.detarver.com

CONTENTS

Preface

Sun Pin is the supposed ancestor of Sun Tzu, if in fact there ever was a Sun Tzu. The ancestral connection could have easily developed through legend and the fact is no one today really knows. That being said, I am not going to go into a long embellished history of Sun Pin's life. It's enough to have his writings and wisdom. There is a lot to be gained by the study of this text. As in the Art of War, this is an interpretation more than a translation. I believe I have made Sun Pin's ideas clear enough that they do not need further explanation.

THE CAPTURE OF PANG CHUAN

Long ago the Governor of Liang sent eighty thousand heavily armored troops led by General Pang Chuan to attack Han tan. When King Wei, ruler of Chi, heard about this he sent eighty thousand of his own heavily armed troops led by his General Tien Ji to defend the border.

When General Chuan attacked the capital of Wei, General Tien Ji asked Sun Pin: "Should I take my men and rush back to their defense?"

Sun Pin said, "No."

General Tain Ji then asked, "What should I do?"

Sun Pin said, "I suggest that we attack the city of Pingling to the south. The city is small, but it controls a large territory, and it has a large population and many armored soldiers. It is a key military town and will be very difficult to conquer, so we may be able to trick them with it. Once we attack, Sung will be to our south, Wei to the north, and Shihchiu will be ahead of us. Since we will have cut ourselves off from supplies, we will appear wholly incompetent.

So the General broke camp and rushed to Pingling, then sent word to Sun Pin asking, "What Now?"

Sun Pin replied, "Of the local rulers, which understand the least about military strategy?"

"Those over in Chicheng and Kaotang." The General answered.

"Give each ruler a small force and have them attack Pang's stronghold. In so doing these two rulers must pass near an open area where there is easy access from all sides, and there are already many armored soldiers and chariots there. Pang will move to attack our two commanders from the rear, but our main force will remain hidden. These two rulers must be sacrificed.

General Tien Chi did as he was instructed and sent the two rulers out on a feeble assault. As predicted, Pang attacked and crushed the two incompetent leaders.

General Tien Chi again summoned Sun Pin and said, "I have followed your instructions and the two rulers have been crushed by Pang's army. What now?"

Sun Pin said, "Send your fastest chariots racing by Pang a few times to anger him. Also send a small force to watch so that he will see them and think our army is small.

General Tien did as instructed, and General Pang became so annoyed that he sent the strength of his military on a forced march to chase down and kill what he thought was the remainder of Tien's army. When Pang's army reached a certain place Sun Pin ordered an attack before Pang's army could rest, and thereby destroyed Pang's army.

At that point everyone understood that Sun Pin was a master of military strategy.

SUN PIN'S DISCOURSE ON MILITARY STRATEGY

In his discussion with King Wei, Sun Pin said, "A wise General does not depend on the use of fixed military positions, this was the way of ancient kings. Victory in war is for the survival of a threatened state, and the protection of its people. Defeat in war means the destruction of property and bondage of the people. For this reason it is vital that one study military strategy.

"Those who abuse their military will fall, and those who use the military for greed and gain will be humiliated. One should take no pleasure in war, nor aim to gain from it.

"Take action only after thorough planning. This way even a small stronghold will be powerful and well supplied. Those who have a small army, yet a strong fighting spirit, will have a moral authority and a keen sense of purpose. No one under Heaven can win a war without being well supplied or without a strong sense of purpose.

"Long ago when Yao ruled the country there were seven instances of rebellion by two tribes in the east and four in the heartland. Yao had no choice but to attack. He crushed the resistance and established his ruler ship over all the land once again.

"History tells us that Shen Nung did battle with the Fu Shi people; the Yellow Emperor did battle with Chih Yu at Shulu; Yao defeated the Kung Kung; Shun attacked Che and drove off the three Miao tribes; Tang banished Chieh; King Wu defeated Chou; and the Duke of Chou destroyed the rebels of Shang.

"Therefore it is said that if one's righteousness is not equal to that of the Five Emperors, then one's ability will not be like that of the Three Kings, and one's wisdom will not be like that of the Duke of Chou.

"One should desire to increase love, spread righteousness, endow the arts and humanities, wear fine clothing, and put an end to conflict and strife. After all this is what Yao and Shun wanted, but even they could not attain it without the use of the military to ensure peace."

THE QUESTIONS OF KING WEI

In Questioning Sun Pin about military strategy, King Wei of Chi asked, "If two armies are evenly matched so that neither general is willing to attack or make the first move, what should be done?"

Sun Pin answered, "Test them with light troops commanded by a brave leader from the lower ranks. Your goal is to distract them, not to gain a victory. While they are distracted, deploy your main force hidden from their sight, and then suddenly attack their flanks. This will bring great success."

King Wei asked, "Are there proper ways to employ large and small scale military forces?"

Sun Pin replied, "There are."

King Wei asked, "If we are stronger and outnumber our opponent, how should we employ our troops?"

Sun pin bowed and said, "This is the question of an enlightened ruler. Even though you are larger and more powerful you still seek the best way to employ your troops. The security of your nation is safe. The proper way is to induce them into attacking. Bring up an auxiliary force and disarray the troops in befuddled formation, so as to appear an easy target for the other side. They will certainly attack."

King Wei asked, "If our opponent is stronger and outnumbers us, how should we employ our troops?"

Sun Pin said, "First insure that your rear is secure so that your army can retreat if necessary. Then send out a smaller advanced strike force and keep your main force hidden. Place the long weapons on the front lines, and the short ones farther to the rear with support from a mobile archer unit. The main body of your force should not move until you have assessed the opponent's full capabilities.

King Wei asked, "How should one attack desperate invaders?"

Sun Pin said, "Wait until they find a way to escape." [A cornered foe can be very vicious.]

King Wei asked, "How should we attack our equals?"

Sun Pin said, "Cause confusion among their ranks and split them up. Use the brunt of your force to strike at part of theirs. If they do not split up, then do not attack. Hold your place and wait. Never attack without full confidence of the situation."

King Wei asked, "Is there a strategy for attacking an army ten times my size?"

Sun Pin said, "Yes. Attack their weakest point when they least expect it."

King Wei asked, "If the ground is level and the troops are well disciplined, but turned back in an assault, what would be the reason?"

Sun Pin said, "It means you lacked a strong frontal attack force."

King Wei asked, "How can I insure that my troops obey every order I give them?"

Sun Pin said, "Every time you give them an order mean it."

King Wei said "Outstanding! You are an excellent military strategist."

General Tien Chi asked, "What troubles the military? What disheartens the opponent? What can make a stronghold impenetrable? Why do we miss Heaven's given opportunities? What causes one to lose the advantage on the battlefield? What causes one to lose favor with the people? May I inquire as to the underlining principles concerning these things?

Sun Pin said, "Terrain is what troubles the military, and cliffs and ravines are what dishearten an opponent. This is why it is said that a mile of marsh will worry an army, because to cross they must leave their heavy artillery behind. So, what causes trouble for the army is terrain, and what disheartens an opponent are cliffs and ravines. If a wall is to be impenetrable it must have a mote and heavy fortifications."

General Tien Chi asked, "Once deployment is underway, what can we do to insure the troops will follow orders?"

Sun Pin said, "You must be stern with orders, but also show them the benefits of following instructions."

General Tien Chi asked, "Would you say the rewards and punishments are the most effective way to control the troops?"

Sun Pin said, "No. Rewards are used to motivate the troops and cause them to fight hard even in the face of death. Punishments are used to maintain order and to cause the troops to show respect to the officers. These can be used effectively to help you win, but they are not the most critical."

General Tien Chi asked, "Would you say then that discipline, strategy, planning, and deception are most critical?"

Sun Pin said, "No. Discipline is used to gather and train an army. Strategy is used to get them to fight hard. Planning is used to thwart an opponent. And deception is used to draw the opponent into a vulnerable position. These also can be used effectively to help you win, but they are not the most critical."

General Tien Chi became flushed and snapped, "Every great general uses these six things to gain victory, and yet you, sir, claim they are not critical. What under heaven is critical then?"

Sun Pin said, "Understanding the opponent, mapping out the battle-ground for advantage, and securing the routes for troop movements and supplies. What is critical to victory is to attack where your opponent is least prepared; these things are most critical."

General Tien Chi asked, "Is there a time when a deployed army should not fight?"

Sun Pin said, "Yes. When you are on a narrow ledge. Increase your fortifications and remain still and quiet. Remain attentive and do not move about. Do not let the opponent lure you, nor let him anger you."

General Tien Chi asked, "How should one engage an opponent larger and better supplied than he?"

Sun Pin said, "Build up your fortifications. Strengthen esprit de corps among your troops and insure they understand your moral authority in the conflict. Run from the opponent to make them arrogant, and make them chase you to exhaust them. Attack where they are not ready, and ambush them when they least expect it. For this type of war you must be ready for a long campaign."

General Tien Chi asked, "What is the best way to use the Awl formation, the Goose formation, and Special Forces. Also how are mobile rapid-fire bowmen best used, and what about the Strong Wind Formation, and the use of foot soldiers?"

Sun Pin said, "The Awl Formation is used for piercing through strong defenses and chipping away at the edges. The Goose Formation is for attacking the flanks and responding to rapid changes. Special Forces are used to penetrate enemy lines and gather information, and for capturing enemy leaders. Mobile rapid-fire bowmen are used to ease the pressure on the front line troops, and for securing a position for a time. A Strong Wind Formation is for a blitz attack. The foot soldiers are used to divide the work and insure victory. But, an enlightened commander never relies on his foot soldiers alone."

After Sun Pin left the discussion, his students asked him about the questions of the King and the General. Sun Pin said, "The King asked about nine matters and the General asked about seven. They are getting close to understanding strategy, but they have not attained enlightenment yet. I have heard it said that those who are honest will find success, as will those who use the military righteously. Also, those who fail to plan properly will suffer, and those who push their troops to exhaustion will fall. Chi will suffer for three generations.

GENERAL TIEN CHI'S QUESTIONS ABOUT STRONGHOLDS

General Tien Chi asked, "When my troops are in the field, how can I have them continually reinforce their strongholds?"

Sun Pin said, "This is a question from an enlightened mind, for this is an area often overlooked or not taken seriously by leaders. There are ways to do this and cause distress to the opponent."

General Tien Chi asked, "Will you tell me about them?"

Sun Pin said, "Certainly. If you employ these tactics you will hold up under stress, and control crucial ground. It is in this way that I captured Pang Chuan."

General Tien Chi said, "That's fine, but these events were long ago, and I still do not understand the strategies."

Sun Pin said, "Caltraps can be used in place of a mote, and wagons can be used as fortified shields. Next use long weapons to keep attackers at bay, use short weapons to support them and to cut off the enemies return. Use long bows as catapults, and keep the center clear for easier maneuverability. Make sure your troops know and understand the plans and tactics that are to be employed.

"The basic rule is, place the long bows next to the caltraps and fire at a pre-determined point. Use bows and spears on a 50/50 basis on the fortifications.

"Another rule is, wait for a report from your spies before you make a move. Set up outposts within sight of each other; on high ground set them up in a box formation, on low ground use a circular formation. Use drums to signal at night and flags to signal by day."

SPECIAL FORCES

Sun Pin said, "Military victory is found in the proper use of Special Forces. Courage is found in righteous authority. Skill is found in strategic formations and training. Readiness is found in trust. Effectiveness is found in strategic planning. Rewards are found in a quick return. Strength is found in giving rest to the troops. Harm is found in prolonged battle.

"Virtue is a warrior's greatest asset. Trust is a warrior's highest reward. Warriors who hate war are of the highest calling. Winning over the people is the first step toward victory.

"There are five major conditions that lead to victory. One who is in command of a fully engaged fighting force will win. One who understands the way of strategy will be victorious. One who wins over the people will be victorious. One whose advisors and command structure are in harmony will be victorious. One who can properly read an opponent's strengths and strategies will be victorious.

"There are five major conditions that lead to defeat. A general who is second-guessed by a king will be defeated. One who does not understand the way of strategy will be defeated. One whose troops do not follow orders will be defeated. One who fails to use spies will be defeated. One who fails to win over the people will be defeated.

"Victory is found in unquestionable trust, a clear system of rewards, selecting strong troops, and taking advantage of an opponent's mistakes. These things are known as a great military treasure.

"A leader with no authority cannot lead.

"There are three traits of a great leader; the first is trust, the second loyalty, and the third is straightforwardness. Loyalty to whom? To the government. Trust in? Trust in a reward system? What straightforwardness? In dealing with evil. Without Loyalty the government cannot empower, without trust in rewards the troops will not fight hard; straightforwardness in dealing with evil will insure discipline.

TIMING STRATEGY

Sun Pin said, "There is nothing more noble under the sun than man. These three things are necessary for a sustained victory, the favor of Heaven, the advantage of terrain, and esprit de corps, without these three things there will be disaster even in victory. Without all three of these one should avoid battle unless there is no other choice.

"Make sure these things are in line, then fight for and secure the peace, and let the troops rest from further war. Those who win battles otherwise do so by the grace of Heaven.

"One who wins six out of ten battles owes his fortune to the stars. One who wins seven out of ten battles owes his fortune to the sun. One who wins eight out of ten battles owes his fortune to the moon. One who wins ten out of ten battles owes his fortune to the skilled officers, but disaster can still arise.

"There are five ways defeat can come, anyone of these five mean you have lost. In the way of strategy there are times when many troops are killed, but the general is not taken. There are times when the officers are killed, but the base camp is left untouched. There are times when the base camp is captured, but the general is not taken, and there are times when the troops as well as the general are killed.

Master the way of strategy and no one can defeat you.

EIGHT COMBAT FORMATIONS

Sun Pin said, "When an ignorant man leads the army he leads by arrogance. When a coward leads the army he leads by boasting. When a man leads the army who does not understand the way of strategy, nor has commanded enough battles to have proper experience, he is surviving on luck.

"Only a leader who fully understands the way of strategy has the wherewithal to secure the borders of a large state, increase the power of the ruler, and create a safe domain for the people. A great leader understands the way of Heaven, he knows the times and conditions of the Earth, the people of the land love him, and he has a complete understanding of his enemy's plans and capabilities. He knows how and when to use each of the eight combat formations, and he only engages an opponent when he knows he will prevail. Otherwise he bides his time. This is a great leader appointed by a wise ruler.

"The use of the eight combat formations is used in accord with the battleground terrain, use whichever one is best suited for the particular conditions of the battle. Deploy a formation in three parts, each with Special Forces in front, and a rear guard. Both should await orders before taking action. Fight with one and defend with the others.

"If the opponent is weak and disoriented send in your Special Forces to take advantage of their condition. If he is strong and disciplined, send in your weaker troops and make him expose himself.

"Divide the chariots and cavalry into three units, one on the right, one on the left, and one to the rear. Use more chariots on easy ground and more cavalry on rugged ground, and use longbows on very difficult ground where neither chariots nor cavalry are suited.

"Regardless of the terrain one should know when to attack and when to defend."

TERRAIN

Sun Pin said, "Terrain that is light is called external, while terrain that is dark is called internal. The light terrain is straight and even while the dark terrain is very dangerous. If you plan according to the terrain, you will not be dismayed. Those on the light ground are safer; those on the dark are in peril.

"As far as the battlefield, the sun is the most important factor, but it is important to remember that the wind can come from any of the eight directions. Bodies of water, hills, the current of a river, deadly ground, and forests should all be considered equally because they all present their own dangers.

"A mountain that sloops toward the south is defensible. A mountain that sloops toward the east is deadly.

"Water flowing toward the east can give life. Water flowing toward the north can take life. Water that does not flow is poison.

"The five types of terrain are in this order. Mountains are greater than high hills, high hills are greater than hills, hills are greater than mounds, mounds are greater than plains, and plains are greater than forests.

"The five notable types of weeds are thorns, brambles, bushes, reeds, and sedge.

"The five types of earth are in this order. Blue is greater than yellow, yellow is greater than black, black is greater than red, red is greater than white, white is greater than blue.

"The five deadly terrains are in this order, gorges, valleys, rivers, marsh, and cliffs. These are natural graves; do not stay on them.

"Do not march down a mountain in the spring. Do not march up a mountain in the fall. Do not send the main part of your troops charging straight into the front right, they should sweep to the right, not to the left."

FORCE AND STRATEGY

Sun Pin said, "Natural weapons like teeth, horns, claws, spurs, and feelings of tranquility when one is happy, and of hostility when one is angry are the natural order of life and cannot be undone. One who is without these natural weapons must use strategy as a means of self-preservation; this is the way of all great leaders.

"The Yellow emperor created the sword, and used it to symbolize battle. Yi created the long bow, and used it to symbolize speed and power. Yu created boats and chariots, and used them to symbolize change. Tang and Wu created spears and long staffs and used them to set a standard for power.

"Now, how do these things symbolize? How does a sword symbolize battle when it is worn days on end without being used? Thus the saying, 'form without substance' is the same as the sword symbolizing battle. No one, no matter how brave, would take a dull sword into battle. And only a fool would lead unfit troops into battle. A sword with no handle is useless, even for the most skilled warrior. Likewise a strike force without a supply line is useless and only a fool would lead them into battle. If a strike force and the rear guard have a solid trust for each other, then the opponent's troops will run from before them.

"Now, how does a bow symbolize speed and power? The arrow is drawn and shot in the distance between the hand and the shoulder, yet it can kill someone more than a hundred paces away so fast that they have no idea where the arrow came from. Hence a bow is speed and power.

"How do boats and chariots symbolize change?....[incomplete]

"How do spears and long staffs symbolize a standard for power? They can attack from high or low and still crush the scull or break the arms. Even those with little skill can use them effectively, thus they set the standard for power.

"Those who understand these four things will win, and those who do not will lose. The way of the military is four fold battle, speed and power, change, and a standard for power. Mastering these four is the way of the general who would destroy opponents and capture kings. Everyone agrees that these four are essential, but no one really understands them."

THE NATURE OF THE MILITARY

Sun Pin said, "If you want to understand the nature of the military, use the bow as a model. The arrows are like troops, the bow like a general, and the archer like a king. The tip of the arrow has sharp metal for killing, and the end has feathers to guide and support. The arrow has heavy armor in the front and light support in the rear, and both must function for the arrow to do its work. Likewise, if you arrange the troops so that they are heavy in the rear and light in the front, they may look fine marching, but they will not kill the enemy, because this arrangement is not like the arrow.

"Now the general is the bow, but if the bow is not gripped in the center when drawn, equal force will not be applied and there will be an imbalance of power. This will bring confusion and the arrow will not hit its target even though the arrow itself is perfect. Thus the general must be in complete harmony with his troops.

"If the arrow is perfect, the bow drawn in perfect balance, but the archer does not aim properly, the arrow will still not hit the target. Even though the military may be in perfect balance, and the general in complete harmony with his troops, if the king is not wise, the military will fail.

"Thus it is said that for the arrow to hit its target all things must work in harmony, so too for the military."

PROPER SELECTION

Sun Pin said, "The proper model for recruiting warriors and energizing people is the balance. With the balance you can separate the best and the brightest. Yin and yang are the means by which one gains the support of the people and attacks the enemy. Make your balance perfect and you will have a standard by which to measure. Evaluate ability and performance against the standard and make appropriate choices.

"Personal and public wealth are the same. There are those with more money than vitality, and there are those with more vitality than money. Only enlightened kings and wise scholars can see this and use it to the best advantage. Those who die under arms will not do so with bitterness, and those who lose their wealth to support the military will not complain.

"In abundant times rules are relaxed and the people will not look to their rulers with respect. In hard times, the people look to their leaders for relief. Tax the people to support the military and your army will always be strong.

Officers

Most of this chapter is missing or corrupt.

Sun Pin said, "Always reward trustworthy officers and don't let anything or anyone corrupt their loyalty. Only send them into battle when you know they will win, but never let them know this. In battle, provide them with support and cover their flanks…"

PROPAGATING ENERGY

Sun Pin said, "When forming an army and assembling troops you should stimulate their energy. When breaking camp and reforming ranks you should keep the troops in order and sharpen their energy. As you approach a border and draw near the enemy you should intensify your troops energy. Once you determine the day for battle you should direct their energy. On the day of battle you should draw out their energy.

"Stimulate their energy by giving them ownership of the mission.

"Sharpen their energy with clear orders.

"Intensify their energy by becoming one of them.

"Direct their energy by making sure each man has three days provisions.

"Sustain their energy by ordering that no food or water be wasted."

LEADERSHIP STRUCTURE

Sun Pin said, "When organizing an army you must set up battle formations, organize and arm troops, and set officers over the troops as appropriate by individual ability. Set the officers apart by use of rank insignia, and set each company of troops apart by use of pennants. Arrange each company by platoon, and each platoon by squad. Organize troops by homeland, and give authority to those who already had authority in their local towns and villages. Disseminate orders by use of gongs and drums. Discipline and unify troops by drill.

"Overwhelm enemy troops by use of long formations, contain them and wear them down.

"Take higher ground and use cloud formations for arrows and spears.

"Surround the enemy using a flowing formation.

"Destroy the enemies advanced guard by cutting them off and closing in on them.

"When going in to rescue stranded troops use a tight formation.

"In heavy battle use alternating squads.

"Employ heavy troops to take a centralized force.

"Employ light troops to take a dispersed force.

"Use a moving formation to take a stronghold.

"Use a square formation on open ground.

"Use an arrowhead formation when taking higher ground.

"Use a circular formation on uneven ground.

"To use troops effectively, continually rotate those on the front lines to the rear guard position for rest.

"Against a disciplined battle line, attack the flanks.

"When you have the enemy trapped offer him a passage to lead him in deeper.

"In thick foliage you need to break out into the open.

"After you have won a battle, keep your troops on alert.

"When training in thick foliage move like a snake, and when exhausted move like a flock of geese. On dangerous ground use every advantage, if you must turn back use the foliage to hide.

"When training around mountain or forest, advance in sections.

"When attacking strongholds, use their water source.

"Train for night retreats and use signals to communicate.

"Use special forces for counter attacks and traps.

"Use the fastest chariots to attack with fire.

"Use arrowhead formations to attack with edge weapons.

"When deploying a small unit use troops highly skilled with various weapons. This is the way to prevent being surrounded.

"Rebuild the ranks and use a standard form of communication to establish solid battle formations.

"Fragmented and interlaced troops frustrate a charging enemy.

"Strong winds and shaky ground cause the opponent uncertainty.

"Hidden and secret schemes will provoke an opponent.

"Crouching Dragons and hidden ambushes are the way to fight in the mountains.

"Strike suddenly and out of nowhere to crush an opponent at a rivers edge, and appear unknowable.

"Use banners in a way to mislead the enemy.

"Pursue a retreating enemy with fast chariots.

"To win against a stronger opponent you must be more agile.

"Trap the enemy with water. Attack him with fire.

"Avoid the enemy and he will chase you.

"Use your special forces to turn away a concentrated attack.

"Highly disciplined troops and strategic formations are key to bringing down enemy strongholds.

"Strategically position your troops and camouflage them to confuse your opponent.

"Intentionally leave behind equipment to bait the opponent.

"Causing heavy causalities will exhaust and unnerve the opponent.

"Relaying orders to guards and patrols verbally is the best way to insure security at night.

"Reward your troops and keep them well supplied and you will see victory. Disciplined and well trained troops are the key to victory."

STRENGTHENING THE MILITARY

Most of this chapter is missing or corrupt, but the essence seems to be:

"Make the state strong, and its military will be strong."

Ten Formations

Sun Pin said, "Generally speaking, there are ten formations used in combat; square, round, scattered, concentrated, arrowhead, hooking, perplexing, fire, and water.

"Use a:

"Square formation to cut off.

"Round formation for strengthening unity.

"Scattered formation for rapid deployment.

"Concentrated formation for defense.

"Arrowhead formation for punching through enemy lines.

"Flanking formation for taking a strong battle line.

"Perplexing formation to confuse the enemy.

"Fire formation to quickly seize enemy encampments.

"Water formation to overrun enemy troops.

"The rule for using a square formation is to thin out the center, thicken the sides, and station Special Forces in the rear. This gives the commander maximum flexibility and striking power.

"The rule for using a scattered formation is that it should be used by light armored divisions with fewer troops. Set up camps of troops with enough distance between them to place numerous fake flags and pennants in order to make your army appear larger than it really is. Set sharp blades at your flanks to keep the enemy from pressing in on you. Chariots should not race and the troops should not run to attack. The idea here is to create many smaller squads, which act separately but as a unit. Some strike while others rest. Some go on the offense while others defend. Some attack from the front, others from the rear or flanks. Some set up ambushes while others attack enemy supply lines. This is how scattered troops can overcome Special Forces.

"The rule for using a concentrated formation is not to allow too much space between the troops. Move about as a unit, weapons ready, the front protecting the rear, the rear protecting the front. If the troops get startled, calm them down. Do not break formation to chase enemy troops, and do not try to prevent the enemy from attacking. Band together and strike down their continuous attacks, or kill their officers. Leave no gaps in your battle line and advance or retreat as one. This way a concentrated formation cannot be overrun.

"Use an Arrowhead formation like a sword. If the tip is not pointed, it will not stab, if the edge is not sharp, it will not cut, and if the base is not sturdy, it cannot be wielded in battle. So make your tip pointed, your edge sharp, and your base sturdy, and then you can use an Arrowhead formation to cut through enemy lines.

"To use a Hooking formation keep the front line straight, and the lines on the left and right hooked. Use gongs, drums, and pipes to send signals. Make sure each section knows its signal.

"To use a perplexing formation a lot of flags and pennants are necessary. If the troops are nervous calm them down. If the chariots are in disarray, put them in order. When the enemy is in place send the troops suddenly thundering forth as though they came out of Heaven, or from the very earth, steady, unwavering, unstoppable, and continuous.

"The rules for the use of fire are: when your moats and ramparts are finished, make more. Set equally sized piles of firewood five paces apart and evenly spaced. Assign specialized troops as fire starters, these should be quick and smart. Make sure you are upwind of the flame, because if you are overwhelmed by smoke in battle you will be destroyed whether you fight or not.

"As a rule of thumb make sure the enemy troops are down wind and that there is plenty of dry grass so they will have nowhere to run. Under these conditions fires can be very effective. Use fire to throw them into chaos and arrows to kill them. Beat drums and make loud noises to motivate your troops. This is the strategy for using fire.

"The rules for fighting an amphibious attacker are: have an abundance of troops and fewer chariots, and make sure the troops are fully equipped. Remain tight when advancing, and spread out when withdrawing. Move with the waters current and target the enemy troops.

"The rules for launching an attack on water are: use smaller boats as guides and faster boats as messengers. Follow a retreating enemy, and close quarters with an advancing enemy. Always be ready to move forward or backward in accord with the opponent. When they move make them doubt their strategy. Strike them as they are setting up their battle line. Divide their troops. Fully arm your troops with every weapon and chariot as needed. Learn the opponent's strengths. Sink their boats, control the fords, and let them know that your troops are imminent. This is amphibious strategy.

Ten Questions

These questions were presented to Sun Pin:

"What if another army equal to ours in everyway comes against us, and both we and they are afraid to make the first move, and they have set camp in a round formation, what should we do?

"In this situation divide your troops into four or five strike force units. Have one unit strike them, but then feign fear and run away. If the opponent believes you are afraid, he will undoubtedly divide his forces and send half out to chase you. While their camp is broken up use drums to signal all and drive your strike force units between his forces and attack in both directions at the same time. When the strike forces unite they will have one purpose and aim. This is how to fight a round formation.

"What if we are attacked by an army superior to us in both money, troops, and supplies, and they take a square formation, what should we do?

"In this situation you should deploy in a scattered formation and hit them until they fragment. Let some attack the front, while others kill them from the rear and they will not know what is going on. This is how to fight a square formation.

"What if we come up against an army of Special Forces that is strong, numerous, motivated, fast and deployed in an arrowhead formation waiting for us, what should we do?

"Divide your troops into three different strike forces. Send one straight in and the other two to their flanks. This will frighten their officers and confuse their troops. Once their formations are in discord, their army is already defeated. This is how to attack an arrowhead formation.

"What if we are already encamped and facing an encamped enemy who has many more powerful troops deployed in a horizontal formation, what should we do?

"Again divide your troops into three strike force units, with one trained as a suicide unit. Send two units to the extended flanks and attack strategic points with the suicide unit. This is the way to kill officers and strike a horizontal formation.

"Suppose we encounter an army with fewer troops, but many more chariots, what should we do?

"Stay on rugged uneven terrain and stay clear of open fields. The open fields are better for the chariots, but the rugged uneven terrain is better for the troops.

"Suppose we encounter an army with many more troops but fewer chariots, what should we do?

"Attack them on open ground, and avoid rugged uneven terrain. Bait them into the open where you will have the advantage even though they have more men and weapons.

"Suppose we encounter an opponent ten times our size and strength, and our supplies have been cut off and our weapons are inferior, but the opponent is pressing us so that we must fight, what should we do?

"To attack an opponent whose men are already occupying superior ground you must find a weakness to exploit before you attack, then pick away at it. Do not be lead into traps.

"Suppose we come against an entrenched enemy who has very brave commanders, superior weapons, and many brave and intelligent troops, and they will not be intimidated because they are well supplied and have a proven strategy, what should we do?

"Make them think you are not committed, appear weak and feeble. Make them think you have already given up. This will cause them arrogance, and will make them lazy and careless. As soon as they put down their guard, strike their weakest point and kill those who are least expecting an attack. This will cause them to move and when they break camp they will be in a hurry and thus be less attentive. Be careful with your timing and strike them at the proper moment, strike as though your army was overly sufficient for the task.

"Suppose we come against an opponent who is imbedded in the mountains and controls all the passes so that we cannot bring reinforcements, but our local troops have no solid ground on which to fight, what should we do?

"You must bait them into the open. Attack vital positions and force them to send reinforcements, and strike them while they are on the move. Set traps and ambushes and distress them until they must come out of hiding, then kill them.

"Suppose we are defending against an aggressive opponent and it appears he has set a trap for us using a basket formation, what should we do?

"Strike them so fast the no one has time to eat or drink. Send two thirds of you troops straight into the attack. When the opponent closes in on them use the remaining one third of your troops to strike their flank. Their army will be in disarray and you can win."

BAITING THE OPPONENT

Most of this chapter is missing or corrupt, but the essence seems to be on baiting your opponent.

AGGRESSORS AND DEFENDERS

In war there are only aggressors and defenders. Aggression is far more costly and requires more resources and men than defense. It is hard for an aggressor to contend without at least twice the men and resources as the defender, because the defender is already set in place and the aggressor must route him out and take his strongholds.

Now, when soldiers would rather face execution than advance on an enemy it can only be because they see the enemy as unbeatable because of military might or unfavorable terrain.

If the military sees their leaders as weak or the battlefield as unfavorable, the troops will hesitate; but if they have confidence in their leaders and the battlefield is favorable, they will be hard to hold back. A wise general will have these things in his favor before he sends his troops to fight.

If you have too many troops in garrison you will not be able to feed them even in a land of abundance. If you have more troops in garrison than in the field, the troops in garrison will grow fat while the troops in the field do without. If you send too few troops out to battle, the enemy will cut them down as they advance.

A wise general knows how to draw and quarter his opponent, and take them out one piece at a time. A general who can divide and conqueror his foes will win even if he has a much smaller army, and a general who cannot will lose even though he may have more strength.

Do you think that just because one has more troops that he will automatically win? If so, just do a head count to determine the victor. Do you think that the richest side will automatically win? If so let the treasurer determine the victor. Do you think that the side with superior weapons and armor will automatically win? If so the victor would always be known before the battle ever started.

Always remember, the rich are not safe simply because they are rich, and the poor are not weak simply because they are poor. The larger do not always win, and the smaller do not always lose. Victory and defeat, and life and death, are determined by each sides motivation and strategy.

When facing a superior force, a general who can divide his opponent's troops, cut their support, neutralize their artillery, or kill their officers can win no matter how brave or strong the enemy's troops are.

The best generals have studied strategy beforehand and thereby achieve victory before troops are deployed. They also maintain victory after the war. The best general's troops will return home unharmed.

SPECIALIST

A specialist can draw and quarter a larger enemies army, cut off their communication, seize their supplies, and control their supply lines. He can destroy one section of the army without the other section having any knowledge of it. A wise specialist can overcome the deepest moats and the highest walls. Neither the fastest chariots nor the sharpest weapons frighten him, and the strongest and bravest warriors are no match for him.

A wise specialist takes control of valleys, and knows every place to set a trap on mountain passes. He loves his men and they know it. They are eager to follow his every command.

He can starve a well-supplied army, and exhaust a resting army. He can cause division among troops that have conquered the world, and quarrels among brothers.

In military operations there are five roads and five movements. They are: Advancing, Withdrawing, Left, Right, and Staying Silently in Place. Specialists know which roads to take and which movements to use so that when they advance they cannot be hit head on, when they retreat they cannot be cut off, when they move left or right they cannot be trapped, and when they stay silently in place they cannot be found. But they frustrate their opponents by heading them off when they advance, cutting off their route when they retreat, and trapping them from the left or right. They can find the enemy no matter how well he hides. They can make the opponent pack up camp and rush here and there to exhaust them, while keeping them too busy to eat or drink.

These specialists defeat armies while their own men eat and rest at leisure. They exhaust armies while their own men play so when the time comes to advance they will not retreat, but they will tread over the sharpest blades without missing a step.

FIVE MILITARY TYPES
FIVE MILITARY COURTESIES

Any army can be one of five types. The first is Intimidating and Fierce. The second is High Headed and Arrogant. The third is Ridged and Unbending. The fourth is Paranoid. The fifth is Slow and Weak.

When contending with an intimidating and fierce force, be humble and yielding.

When contending with a hoity and arrogant force, be courteous and patient.

When contending with a ridged and unbending force, be clever and bait them.

When contending with a paranoid force, draw their attention to their front and strike their flank, deepen your moats and strengthen your walls, and then seize their supplies.

When contending with a slow and weak force, unsettle them with terror, and unnerve them. If they move strike them, if they do not move surround them.

An army can use any of the five guidelines for tender actions or any of the five guidelines for forceful actions. What are the guidelines for the five tender actions?

1. If an army invades a forgiven land and is too tender it will lose its initiative.
2. If an army invades a foreign land a second time and is too tender it will lose its incentive.
3. If an army invades a foreign land a third time and is too tender it will lose its own supplies.
4. If an army invades a foreign land a forth time and is too tender it will lose its food.

5. If an army invades a foreign land a fifth time and is too tender it will lose its objective.

The guidelines for the five forceful actions are.

1. If an army invades a foreign land with too much force it will be called barbaric.

2. If an army invades a foreign land with too much force a second time it will be called arrogant.

3. If an army invades a foreign land with too much force a third time it will be called terrorist.

4. If an army invades a foreign land with too much force a fourth time it will be called deceived.

5. If an army invades a foreign land with too much force a fifth time it will be called exhausted.

Always remember that tenderness and force must be properly balanced for maximum effect.

MILITARY BLUNDERS

If you rely solely on using a people's insecurity to wear down their army, you will wear down your own army.

If you try to build up your state's strengths to match the strengths of the enemies state, you will inhibit your army.

If your strongholds offer little resistance against enemy artillery, your whole army will be disregarded.

If your artillery is ineffective against enemy strongholds, your whole army will be disregarded.

If an army is skilled at deployment and unit rotation, and knows the terrain, but still cannot obtain victory, then their leaders do not understand the difference between Civil Victory and Military Victory.

If a seemingly strong army cannot obtain great victories it is because their leaders do not understand initiative.

If an army loses the support of the people, it is because their leaders do not understand excess.

If an army applies maximum force but still accomplishes little, it is because their leaders do not understand timing.

If an army cannot settle continuing problems, it is because their leaders do not know how to inspire the people.

An army that suffers regret has followed corrupt leaders.

If an army cannot avoid coming disaster, or take advantage of developing opportunities, it is because their leaders are not prepared.

If an army does not seize the opportunity to do good, misses the time to take action, and cannot keep evil down, then they are going nowhere.

If an army controls its power and behaves in a kind and respectful way, is courteous even when it is unnecessary, is gentle yet powerful, and is strict yet flexible, it is going to flourish.

If you take the road to nowhere nothing in Heaven or Earth will stop your destruction.

If you take the road toward flourishing Heaven and Earth will insist on your prosperity.

RIGHTEOUS LEADERS

Leaders must be righteous. If not they will not be respected. If they are not respected they will not be loved. If they are not loved their troops will not lay their lives on the line for them. Thus righteousness leads the military.

Leaders must love their troops. If not their troops will not love them. If their troops do not love them they will not fight hard. Thus love is the heart of the military.

Leaders must be moral. If not they will have no authority. If they have no authority they cannot inspire their troops. Thus morality is the arms of the military.

Leaders must be honest. If they are not they will not be trusted and their orders will not be obeyed. If their orders are not obeyed, their troops will not rally. If their troops do not rally they will not survive. Thus honesty is the legs of the military.

Leaders must be wise. If not they will be second guessed. Thus wisdom is the backbone of the military.

EFFECTIVE LEADERS

This section is too fragmented to really interpret, but the essence seems to be:

A leader should love his troops as he does his own children, and train them like a stern teacher.

DEFEATED LEADERS

These things can cause a leader to fail.

If his ego makes him think that he is capable of more then he really is.
If he is arrogant,
If he is power hungry,
If he is greedy,
…,
If he is impetuous,
If he is slow,
If he is a coward,
If he is courageous but weak,
If he is untrustworthy,
…,
…,
…,
If he is indecisive,
If he is too relaxed,
If he is slothful,
If he is overbearing,
If he is cruel,
If he is selfish,
If he is in disorder.

The more of these a leader suffers from the less effective he will be.

LOSING LEADERS

These things will always cause a leader to lose.

If he loses his drive,
If he gathers base men and straightway uses them as his army,
If he captures retreating troops and immediately sends them in to fight for
his cause,
If he assumes he has everything necessary for battle, but does not.
If he continuously struggles over right and wrong, or contends over strategy,
If his orders are not followed and his men lack esprit de corps,
If his junior officers are rebellious and his men unwilling to fight,
If the people hate his army,
If his troops are worn out,
If his troops are not committed,
If his troops desert,
If his troops are undisciplined,
If his troops are easily frightened,
If his troops are unwilling to suffer whatever is necessary to obtain victory,
If his troops are exhausted from building strongholds,
If he is unprepared for battle,
If his troops lose heart because of long marches to the battlefield,
…,
If his troops are terrified,
If his commands are constantly changing and his troops procrastinate,
If his troops do not have esprit de corps, nor faith in their leaders,
If the troops have had no real challenge and become complacent,
If there are a lot of rumors that cause his troops to doubt him,
If he cannot take correction,
If he has appointed less capable leaders,
If he draws out an engagement so long that his troops become unmotivated,

If he sends his troops into battle before they are unified,

If he relies on the weakness of the opponent,

If he is a liar, a sneak, or enjoys cruelty,

If he is unconcerned for the welfare of his men,

If his artillery and troops do no mutually trust one another,

If in the heat of battle he focuses only on the front lines and leaves the rear unguarded, or focuses on the rearguard and leaves the front weak, or focuses on the left or right flank so that the other is weakened, or if his mind is consumed with worry during battle.

STRONG AND FEEBLE CITIES

Strong Cities

If a city is situated in a marsh and has no mountains or canyons, but has built up mounds on all four corners, it is too strong to attack.

If a city has its own fresh water source, it is too strong to attack.

If a city is situated half way up a mountain so that there is a steep slope before it and a mountain peak behind it, it is too strong to be attacked.

If a city is built around high ground that peaks in the center, it is too strong to be attacked.

Feeble Cities

An army that is tired enough to rest by a rushing river has lost its energy and desire and is weak and can be taken.

A city that is situated with its back to a canyon and has no mountains protecting its sides is weak and can be taken.

A city situated on a dry wasteland is weak and can be taken.

If troops have nothing but stagnant water to drink, they are weak and can be taken.

A city situated in a large marsh with no hills or valleys is weak and can be taken.

A city situated between mountains with no canyons or mounds is weak and can be taken.

A city situated with a large mountain before it and a deep canyon behind it is weak and can be taken.

PROPER STRATEGY

If a cornered foe requests reinforcements they can be destroyed when they arrive. It is a general principle that units at least fifteen miles apart cannot help each other much less units a hundred miles or more apart, these are the extreme.

As a rule of thumb, do not engage your opponent in a long campaign if he is far better supplied than you.

If his troops severely outnumber yours, do not engage him on the battlefield.

If your troops are not trained and armed, at least as well as your opponent's, do not fight him head to head.

Once you have a thorough understanding of these things you should plan your strategy to include the following.

1. Seize their supplies and provisions.
2. Seize their water source.
3. Control the fords.
4. Control the roads.
5. Control the valleys.
6. Control the battlefield.
7. ...
8. ...
9. Seize their most prized valuables.

These are the nine steps to controlling the enemy.

FLEXIBILITY

All things being equal, the concentrated will defeat the scattered, the full will triumph over the empty, the fast will win over the slow, and the large will defeat the small, and the rested will destroy the exhausted.

There is a time and a place for every military strategy. Concentrate when it is necessary to concentrate, scatter when it is necessary to scatter, fill up when it is necessary to be full, and empty when it is necessary to be empty. Take shortcuts when it is reasonable to take shortcuts. Use major highways and roads when it is reasonable to use them. Go fast when it is necessary to go fast, and go slow when it is necessary to go slow. Gather large armies when it is necessary to have large armies, and deploy in small units when it is necessary to fight in smaller units. Rest at the proper time and work at the proper time.

Be flexible with your strategy. Be ready to go from concentrated to scattered, from full to empty, from back roads to highways, from fast to slow, from large to small, and from resting to working.

Outsmart your opponent. Do not attack the concentrated with the concentrated, the scattered with the scattered, the full with the full, or the empty with the empty. Do not attack the fast with the fast, the slow with the slow, the large with the large, or the small with the small. Do not attack the resting when you should be resting, nor the exhausted when you are exhausted.

Concentrate to fight a scattered opponent. Be full to fight an empty opponent. Use shortcuts to fight an opponent on the highways. Be fast to fight a slow opponent. Be large to fight a small opponent. Be fresh to fight an exhausted opponent.

CONVENTIONAL AND UNCONVENTIONAL WARFARE

It is the way of Heaven and earth to vacillate from one extreme to the other like the Sun moving from east to west, the Yin and the Yang. From abundance to death, the seasons are an example. From victory to defeat there are five places. There is living and dying, the capable and the incapable, and surplus and famine.

Any foe that can be seen can be defeated. The strategist uses well thought out strategy to win, and strategy is never ending. In contending for victory a strategist must be ever vigilant to the instant changes in war because there is no single superior strategy in any given conflict. Therefore a single army must have many plans.

A wise strategist knows his opponents strengths and weaknesses, and where he is lacking and where he is abundant. He can clearly see victory before engagement as clearly as the result of pouring water on a fire.

To attack power with power head on is conventional, to control power through manipulation is unconventional, and the combinations of these two things are endless. Once you know your opponent you can plan your strategy.

Armies that are equal are not set to obtain victory one over the other. You should strive to make the armies unequal. Be still when the opponent is moving, be fresh when he is exhausted, be full when he is empty, disciplined when he is unordered, large when he is small, and then take the initiative and attack. He who controls the element of surprise will win the battle.

If one joint is injured, all the joints rest, because they are of the same body. Likewise, if the frontline is destroyed the rear guard is useless because they are the same body. For power, the unit must hold its shape, the rear should crowd the front and the front should not step on the rear. There should be a plan for advancing and a plan for withdrawing.

Use rewards to lead your troops and they will obey your orders. If the rewards are high and the punishments are harsh and the troops still do not fulfill their orders, then the orders are impossible to fulfill. To lead troops in such a way as to have them face death without fleeing, in spite of poor officers, is something that every great general finds difficult. To require this of regular troops is like trying to reverse the flow of a river.

To be a great leader you should reward the achievers, replace the weak, give rest to the exhausted, and food to the hungry. Build an army that will face the enemy to the death without running. A tidal wave can sweep away boulders and break ships in two. Likewise a well-constructed army that employs its troops by their natural talents will carry out commands with the power of a tidal wave.

AFTERWORD

I think of all the important lessons in Sun Tzu's and Sun Pin's work, the parts on how to treat your own people are probably the most important. Let's face it. If you are not treating your own people right, you have bigger problems than how you're going to gain the next mile. Your biggest concern should be how to keep from losing what you already have.

People are people in every age, career, and walk of life. It takes basically the same strategy to motivate little Johnny to clean his room as it does to get a foreign leader to sign a peace accord. People just don't vary that much.

A friend of mine said that his basic approach to every walk of business is, "Do the right thing." That struck close to home for me, and seems to sum up most of Sun Tzu's and Sun Pin's teaching on running an organization. When you get right down to it, doing the right thing for a Marine, employee, soldier, or family member is doing that which will strengthen the Corps, organization, military or family. Often doing the right thing is not the easy choice, but it is always the best choice.

You should conduct your business as though your every motivation was open for everyone to see. If you do everything in the open and with complete integrity, people will know this and will trust your word even if they don't like it.

Good luck in your endeavor. If you are part of the military, God Bless you. We need and appreciate you more than you know.

D.E. Tarver

ABOUT THE AUTHOR

D. E. Tarver holds black belts ranging from 2nd to 7th degree in seven different styles of Japanese and Filipino martial arts. He has taught martial arts and strategy for twenty years. He produced and starred in the very popular, "The Dojo Floor", a thirteen-episode show on various aspects of martial arts. He joined the National Guard at the age of 17 with his parent's permission, and then transferred to the United States Marine Corps at the height of the Iran hostage crisis. Since his honorable discharge from the Marines, he has spent time in Japan and the United States.

0-595-22472-5

Printed in the USA
CPSIA information can be obtained
at www.ICGtesting.com
LVHW041131071223
765754LV00001B/136

9 780595 224722